INNATE INDEPENDENCE
REPOSITIONING THROUGH THE MIND OF RESILIENCE

PETA COLLETT

 A catalogue record for this book is available from the National Library of Australia

Copyright © 2020 Peta Collett

All rights reserved worldwide.

No part of the book may be copied or changed in any format, sold, or used in a way other than what is outlined in this book, under any circumstances, without the prior written permission of the publisher.

Publisher:
Inspiring Publishers
P.O. Box 159, Calwell, ACT Australia 2905
Email: publishaspg@gmail.com
http://www.inspiringpublishers.com
National Library of Australia Cataloguing-in-Publication entry

Author: Collett, Peta

Title: **INNATE INDEPENDENCE:**
   Repositioning Through the Mind of Resilience/Peta Collett.

ISBN: 978-1-925908-88-6 (Print)
ISBN: 978-1-925908-89-3 (eBook)
ISBN: 978-1-922327-49-9 (Hardcover)

About the Author

People are saturated in diagnostic labels, therapy sessions, over medicated, stressed more than ever, and have forgotten how resilient self- enabling and emotionally smart they are. Learn how to create a mind that thrives on challenge and how to switch to a more confident you.

Switching it all off and switching it all on again can help you discover your natural keys to a healthier mind and more confident you by applying practical steps.

After years of major depression, anxiety and eating disorders, I learnt how to create greater self-confidence by using imagination, creativity, structured thinking and how to develop problem solving skills.

Developing good mind esteem without professional supports, minimal social supports and medications taught me how to problem solve, develop inner strength and resilience independently.

You are what you eat, you're also what you think you are.

Thank you to wonderful friends and people I've met that enjoy sharing their challenges.

Peta Collett

Table of Contents

About the Author 3

Racing Thoughts 7

Scrambled Egg Brain 10

Simple Retraining 12

Calming Thoughts of the Mind 20

Challenging Beliefs 24

Creating Individual Order 27

The Great Comparison 29

Understanding Satisfaction 32

The Calming Influence of Satisfaction 36

Having Enough 41

Mastering the Anxious Mind 44

Take a Deep Breath and Chill 51

The Negative Mindset 53

Redirecting Chaotic Thoughts..56

Reducing Tension and Creating Physical Calm.................59

The Master in the Ear..65

The Art of Empowering Self-Praise..67

A Ray of Sunshine..70

The Driver of Dreams and Visions...84

Exchange of Language and Building Friendships...............89

Shifting Through the Brain Gears..92

The Quest of Self-Love..93

Simple Re-affirming Thoughts..99

Music Fulfills and Motivates the Soul..................................102

Increase Your Imagination...104

Racing Thoughts

I'm sure you've noticed our world is full of what looks like and sounds like a volcano of information overload. A volcano about to erupt I might add. Perhaps you have a completely different definition of overload. You may have noticed your digital world fills quickly with ads, updates, instalments etc. It's possible to describe an overload of electronic movement that filters through our laptops, news feeds, and mobile phones as an assault on the senses. Let's not forget the large flashing billboards that adorn the side of city commercial sites etc, all competing to get our attention.

It's exhausting at times as your brain can feel overloaded, your mind can feel chaotic as it's sorting through the information. Your brain can get to a point where you feel addicted to technology, scrolling the pages quickly as your fingers move faster than lightening. Yep, your mind is racing as it scans over information quickly looking for something to satisfy itself. Sound familiar? Let me explain in simple terms how you can find tranquil places to sift through all the information, regain your own thoughts and travel on your own path of discovery or self-discovery to a calmer brain. Just for a moment. Switch it all off.

Have you ever had a mind that felt like it was racing? If you use social media, then I'm sure you are familiar with the overload of information that can filter through your pages very quickly. You may not even utilise much of the internet or digital technology and still feel like you are wallowing in an overload of thought processes like road maps. Overwhelming thoughts without a specific direction or any sense of order I might add. What would happen if you could create a visualisation of what racing thoughts might look like? Perhaps I can help you.

If you've ever looked at a road map without using the key codes to help you define your journey, then you will know exactly what I'm referring to. Perhaps you've travelled abroad and stood in a multileveled train station and looked at the maps of train tracks that lead to hundreds of suburbs, not knowing which railway line your destination is on. Suddenly the foot traffic speeds up through the station as peak hour ascends. You panic knowing you are standing in the way as crowds of grey suits speed past you as the many corporate workers rush to get home. There isn't anyone working at the station available close by to ask and your appointment time draws closer. After a while you brave the flow of corporate workers rushing towards their destination and ask for directions, "No idea," the first responds. "Sorry, can't help," the second replies. The third person notices you but deliberately looks at their watch to indicate they don't have time to answer your query. You brave walking against the flow of traffic to cut through the queues of human peak hour traffic and look for a railway employee to ask for directions. You can feel your body becoming very flustered and your head is thinking less clear. Your mind has a quick visual of the large board with all the red, yellow, green, and blue lines listed heading towards hundreds of suburbs. You gasp as you know you are unable to make sense of the railway map within the limited time frame you have. You're still searching trying to find someone to help. Ah, finally you see a railway worker.

You ask, for directions, "Can you please tell me which train to Lincoln?"

"Level 23, 4 will be visible on the front of the train and the next is in 6 minutes," is the response.

"Thank you very much," is your panicked sounding reply.

Suddenly you turn around feeling very panicked at the thought of your train leaving in six minutes time.

You squeeze in to join the queue of grey suits rushing to various platforms. You arrive in time, take a deep breath, and feel your body relax a little knowing you boarded the train. You then decide to take note of the smaller poster on the train carriage wall with all the suburbs and which platform station you will need to exit the train. You start to feel a little more orientated, you notice your breathing reduce its heaviness and your thoughts have slowed down as you count 18 stops before your station. As you start to relax a little more, you giggle to yourself and think, "Next time I'll just ask someone to help straight up before I waste time reading railway maps on my own in a multi- level train station."

Scrambled Egg Brain

Perhaps your mind struggles with something other than racing thoughts. Some days your mind feels like scrambled eggs. Your mind feels like eggs that were cracked into the pan with the purpose of being a perfectly round white with a lovely yellow centre, intended for the top of a beautiful green lettuce salad, go south. Unfortunately, the eggs didn't take the form you expected and start to run into each other turning into scrambled eggs. Just like scrambled eggs your structured thinking how you will go about your day and what you need to achieve seem to have gone completely south. You struggle to maintain your sense of order; you suddenly realise that you need to work hard to focus without the distractions of intruding thoughts.

You start to feel panicked as you know you are struggling to focus. You feel your mind is about to shut down completely. It's scrambled egg brain and racing thoughts that leave you feeling you lack so much peace in yourself. How can you move your thoughts from scrambled egg mode into some sort of order? Well, I've got to say it's not impossible and learning to create order is achievable.

Firstly, take a deep breath, take the time to turn off every distraction. Just chill for a moment before redirecting your thoughts.

If you continually struggle with scrambled egg brain, try writing a list of small tasks to complete each day or week and make yourself determined to finish tasks. You can write down, verbalise, or create other ways to express some of those intruding thoughts or lack of connected ideas. You can learn to manage, minimise, and restructure your thoughts. Whatever method you chose you can develop and maintain a powerful sense of ordered thought life if you chose to.

During the years of thought re-structuring, I often used self-affirmations. Self-affirmations can be powerful for re-creating your thought life. E.g. "I can do this," or, "I can get it together." Speaking to your mind is a helpful tool, "Ok brain, let's get happening today," or, "Ok, I'm not going to get distracted." If verbalising self-affirmation recalls a picture of that old derelict man yelling as he pushes his cart along the street, you might like to re-think that. Developing a self-affirmation love language with your brain is a good thing. Telling your mind to calm down or slow down can send messages to the rest of your body, and can have a more calming effect on your body. I know from years of depression and anxiety, that you can practice a calmer brain without medications by practicing being aware of what your mind is doing.

It's helpful to write down, verbalise, doodle, or find other ways to express unproductive thoughts to help manage and minimise. Always remember it's all about managing then minimising.

Simple Retraining

Retraining your mind isn't rocket science. Working to time frames can be successful if you persevere. Oh yeah, I get it, if you're a creative or someone who doesn't like anything that reminds you of pressure from that nagging parent, school- teacher or employer I completely understand. Whatever the reason, just try and think positively about it all for a few moments.

Let's face it, we live in a society that is overdriven by Key performance indicators, production timelines, all kinds of pressures, etc. However, retraining your mind to time frames, even working to small time frames is a helpful motivator. Try to make retraining enjoyable for yourself. For example, try a simple task that you enjoy, work on it slowly in brief time frames over a few days. Get into the habit of completing a physical job or healthy self-affirming thought process. Celebrate when you complete your task. If catching up with friends is your thing or going on journeys or whatever it is, practice finishing what you start. It helps the brain re-create a system of order.

I remember feeling very unsettled and unable to complete tasks. It may seem strange; however, in my journey of reconnecting my mind to focus on a task for a long time, I sat tirelessly for days reading and deleting emails after returning from holidays. Why didn't I just hit the delete button on all my junk mail you ask? Well, I chose to persevere with the most tedious task to start to retrain my mind to focus on completing small tasks, then completing small jobs, eventually building up to more significant tasks. One of my greatest flaws was not completing projects. My mind would do the scrambled egg thing, and I'd find myself doing everything in the form of distraction. I might as well have said, "Distraction come on down!" like a prize-winning contestant show calling out the next candidate. Eventually, I learned to create order on all kinds of levels.

If you struggle with focus, try something small to begin with. I'm sure you've heard of UFO's, oh and that's not those giant silver spaceships flying in the sky with little green men. UFO stands for Unfinished Objects. Learn to complete the simplest of tasks, don't give in to negative thoughts.

They can sound like, "What's the point? I can't be bothered. No one notices, no one listens, no one cares," and so on. Learning to change negative thoughts will help you increase your productivity from smaller tasks to more significant tasks. I've completed many projects, not necessarily because they thrilled me but more so because I knew it was good for my self-esteem and training of my mind. Working to a time frame can increase motivation and can be used as a pivotal point at later stages in your life. You can look back knowing you completed something, and you had the motivation to do so.

Learn to recognise what motivates you and what you want. Many years ago, I sat my final nursing exams holding a screaming newborn. Not the ideal situation, however that experience has been a place my mind has pivoted back to on many occasions to top up my internal perseverance and resilience levels. Motivation for me at that point in life was a qualification and the fact people didn't think that I could achieve.

Take time to understand something of how your brain works. Understanding your brain doesn't mean you need to know about all the neurons in the brain, let's face it that would take forever as the brain has billions of neurons. However, you can take time to understand what type of learner you are.

Are you a Visual (Spatial); an Aural (Auditory-Musical); a Verbal (Linguistic); a Physical (Kinaesthetic); a Logical (Mathematical); Solitary (Intrapersonal); or Social (Interpersonal). These terms may sound unfamiliar if you're not used to them? E.g. A visual learner requires to be shown instructions or uses colour, illustration etc. An Aural learner digests information from engaging in conversations, listening to audio, videos etc. Do you remember learning to ride a bike? That was part of Physical Learning, your ability developed through a hands-on approach. If you love maths, exploring how systems work and how they fit big picture thinking, then designing shoes could be your thing.

Only kidding about the shoe part; however, the business of shoes requires plenty of logical thinkers. Solitary learners thrive best when working things out on their own and Social Learners love sharing and learning in group dynamics. Do I believe people fit into one category? Absolutely not. I'm inclined to think people change their learning styles at various stages of their lives.

Two of the most overused questions young people get asked are, "What do you want to do?" and, "What do you want to be?" Both these questions create unnecessary stress. Young people don't need the pressure of feeling like their future needs to be completely mapped out and boxed with a specific role or learning style. Realistically, global economics change for a whole bunch of reasons, the job market changes, and so does the need to be adaptable. Perhaps, "Where would you like to start?" is less stress-provoking.

Why allow yourself the boxing of labels and specific learning styles? I often say to young people, find things to do that you enjoy, be involved in the community, and learn skills that occupy your mind until you work out a career direction. Let's face it, some people aren't career driven and that's o.k. too.

O.K. back to learning styles. If your brain is quite brilliant and filled with potential unlocked grandiose dreams, you may be a visual learner. If your brain feels like it's scattered out in another galaxy somewhere, or floating in the ocean between the sandy shores and the sunset settling, perhaps you are a logical thinker, destined to make boats or spacecraft. Unless you explore your learning style, make some plans, and make a start, you will never know how capable your mind is. Asking yourself questions helps you determine where your intelligence is at and what types of learning styles will help you achieve your goals in life. O.K., the part about the ocean and the sunset might help you identify as an abstract thinker or just the fact you wish you were at sea.

If you have struggled with depression, racing thoughts or scrambled egg brain and how it affects you, you are not alone. I have met very few people who have never experienced dark thought spaces, anxiety, racing thoughts or self-confidence challenges.

You might relate to the following description of racing thoughts or have a completely different narrative. Racing thoughts have a life of their own; they can move quickly like an influx of conversations bouncing off lips, communications that seem to jump from one topic to the next without consistent connection. Racing thoughts can move through your mind faster than an Interstate passenger rail train. As you try to verbalise what you think sounds like your passionate sounding conversation, it leaves the audience stunned as they struggle to make connections between one paragraph to the next.

You may have encountered that blank expression from someone that says no-one is home as they stare at you, because you just blurted out all kinds of disconnected sentences.

I'm sure you've encountered that blank expression from someone that says no-one is home as they stare at you, because you just blurted out all kinds of sentences.

If you are struggling with racing thoughts, find a space free from distractions, just for a moment relax from the flurry of thought processes, yes, a deep breath or sigh right about now would be ideal.

Just for a moment, take yourself somewhere quiet, soothing and ponder about what you need. Being in the habit of switching off from the pressures of the world is a crucial key to a calmer mind. Identifying what your thoughts look and sound like can help in the process of creating a language to express and retrain them.

Just for a moment, switch off technology and all the surrounding noise if possible and take time to listen to your thoughts.

Identifying what your thoughts look and sound like can help express and rearrange them into something calmer, then a sense of order. Remember the learning styles I mentioned earlier? You may find you rearrange racing thoughts while doing things as you start to become anxious. Write them down, doodle them, sketch them, verbalise them, talk them out, create music, use a deck of cards, swim, play with a rubric cube, whatever floats your boat. Try exploring ways of expressing and rearranging thoughts. You don't necessarily need to be sitting on the floor with your legs crossed meditating to switch your mind to another station. We all experience anxiety at times; it's O.K. the more you learn to manage and minimise the more clarity you will have.

I'm sure; you're aware the brain doesn't filter decision making when stressed, overworked, and lacking sleep. Next time you require sleep, take note of the smaller details your mind misses in the following day. You might skip details in paperwork, don't stop at the red traffic light, feel irritable or continually miss appointments. These are times your brain is not functioning at its best; take note of areas you need to focus on more than usual. Catnaps and small breaks can make a difference in your brain functioning.

The brain goes into overdrive and burns itself out when we are stressed or overworked. Your motivation will eventually change as your functioning in day to day work and activities will decrease. Eventually you will start to think a whole bunch of negative thoughts. "I can't be bothered," and, "I don't care," will slide themselves into your thought processes like Cinderella's foot gliding into a glass slipper. Unfortunately, it's really the Ugly Stepsisters trying to steal the glass slipper and glam up a pair of feet that just don't fit the slipper.

The cycle of the racing mind burns out then leads into depression. People get panicky as they aren't keeping up and so on. Suddenly we don't listen, we find it hard to follow instruction and a cycle of negative self-absorption starts. Learn the patterns of overdrive and what the underlying motive is that drives you. Overly ambitious people tend to burn themselves out a lot quicker than other people. People tend to burn out because they take too much on. Learn to say NO, people will always find someone else to do the job. If you learn to recognise the thinking processes you will manage, minimise and heal.

Calming Thoughts of the Mind

Nature is an amazing place to be in and switch off from the pressures of the world. A beautiful landscape isn't generally intrusive, doesn't want to talk us down, argue with us or create stress by acting contentious towards us. A stunning seascape doesn't want to sell or promote anything other than its natural splendour. Climate change and natural disasters are the exception to the balance of nature. We also need to consider where we go in certain environments due to their sacredness.

In contrast to nature, technology has led us to living in apartments and hotel rooms without natural light and with artificial plant life. Not only do we carry our phones, switch on our computers, overuse so many digital devices, we have created a synthetic world void of individualised touch.

So much of nature is soothing, with lots of green to explore when walking through rain forests, and the touch of your hand on beautiful green foliage still dewy from the cold evening air. We can still enjoy natural environments filled with greens of varying tones; the colour associated with calm and peace. Perhaps you live close enough to an ocean and allow the waves of the ocean to roll over you and feel the sand between your toes. If so then you have just experienced the most fabulous spa bath under the heavens. Your body feels invigorated and alive as you walk out of the ocean ready to take on a new adventure. Perhaps you have somewhere else you feel calm in nature or somewhere you would like to explore. Where would we be without nature?

We need to feel calm to increase our awareness of self and others around us, to improve our intelligence. The mind relaxes when we feel calm, our posture changes resulting in less adrenalin running through our bodies. Our complexion changes radiating a healthier glow as blood flows through capillaries closer to the skin. As our inner person relaxes, we generate a beautiful peace through our whole being. If you are an experienced meditator or someone who knows how to completely switch off, then you would have experienced the following:

Completely relaxed is completely detached, you do not feel emotionally pressured, you will not feel any type of physical connection to yourself or others. You will need to orientate yourself once you have finished a switched off state. It is the most liberating beautiful experience when completely burden free. We generate an approachable atmosphere around us. We are our most powerful when we are calm. We can think how to defend ourselves; we are able to heal ourselves; we are able to define ourselves because we are calm enough in our thoughts to think things through. We have the capacity to make good decisions for ourselves and others in our care. We are also very loveable when we are at our calmest.

Just sit or lay down quietly for a moment and allow your mind to take you somewhere you feel calm enough to enhance you in this beautiful journey. Consider how your body feels with a massage, bath, or something you find relaxing. Take note of the expression on your face, how your body feels and how you feel emotionally. As much as the body enjoys time to destress, your mind does also.

If you can't physically connect with your calming natural environment right now, perhaps you can just imagine being there.

Ah, hopefully you feel a little more relaxed and I hope your mind is rested a little. Now, where were we? Yes, hmmm, the quest, the vision, the horizon perhaps, the conversation and connecting all the dots together in your quest of creating a calm mind. Before we go any further, perhaps you could ponder on these thoughts about diagnosis and mind esteem.

Challenging Beliefs

Have, you noticed that so many behaviours today have a diagnosis? What seemed like normal behaviour or even a little eccentric behaviour once upon a time now has a diagnosis. Interesting to note, not only do we explore action somehow, we seem to give so many responses a label and medicate it. Over the years, I've had conversations with parents about children who were entrepreneurial or creatives but labelled as difficult. I remember children who didn't want to participate in the same activities as other children when asked to and classed as having learning or behavioural problems. Is it possible we accept the diagnosis or label too quickly sometimes rather than exploring our options? How many times have you heard of someone or had a prescribed script that you just didn't need or wasn't right for you? I've wondered at times what types of labels and medications I would be taking if I'd pursued support through professional networks.

When I was a child, I counted syllables constantly in my mind. Each time I heard a conversation or thought about a sentence, I would break the sentence down into syllables and count them. A somewhat compulsive habit to develop in my mind which almost drove me insane by the way. Eventually the habit faded away as my mind started to focus on other more important things, like which coloured pencils, I should create beautiful illustrations with. Anyway, you may be familiar with the diagnosis, Obsessive Compulsive Disorder. People live with OCD and carry out all kinds of ritualistic behaviours, which make sense to them or feel they don't have control over their behaviours. People in previous times were known to avoid blasphemous thoughts with all kinds of practices. Not that I was too concerned with blasphemous thoughts at age ten. In my case it was my inability to resolve numerical counting patterns of syllables. As my thinking started to evolve, so did my ability to put numbers into music, art, design etc. You can google information or find books on OCD; you may be surprised at some of the awful treatments of OCD and supposed causes. OCD has a long history associated with religious beliefs and paranoias attached to it. However, this narrative is not intended to label, diagnose, or leave you feeling like there is something wrong with you. This narrative is to encourage you to explore unproductive thinking and find ways to master your thought processes.

You may be a creative person who works intuitively, however if you were to apply principles of mathematics you would discover creativity is made up of composition, proportion and is mathematically based.

Years later in my adult years I realised through a conversation with another adult, that counting is the foundation of music, which of course you would know if you were a musician that music is numerically based. Of course, that little snippet of information helped explain my mind counting syllables. Perhaps if I'd shared my counting obsession someone could have picked up on it and synced a few cool rhythms with me. Perhaps you counted constantly or have a habitual habit?

If you're not a musician and you tapped your fingers or feet to one of your favourite tunes and stopped to think about it, you would realise you were moving in a rhythm of numbers. Try it the next time you hear a cool song or music composition.

Perhaps the next time you are diagnosed with something give yourself the time to question if the diagnosis fits. Take some time to think about any thought patterns and behaviours you have developed and how they could be influencing your mind and what you need to do to change them or improve them. People can grow out of obsessive behaviours by challenging their thought processes.

Creating Individual Order

Most of what we do in life revolves around systems of order. Perhaps you're an abstract thinker that relies on other people to fill the details in to help complete and communicate the bigger picture. If you were an abstract artist for example, then you probably know that foundation rules are learned and then broken or stretched out or whatever other term you chose to use. What looks like a distorted view of an art piece to someone without any understanding of art, may be very logical to someone with an understanding of art.

My point is, it can feel effortless to look at an individual that behaves in a way that doesn't seem logical or follow the same working patterns of order as others. However, the individual may be following some sort of pattern that makes perfect sense to them. Looking back at counting syllabus in my mind didn't seem logical at the time. Counting syllables felt very isolating, however sharing thoughts with others can help gain perspective and manage thinking patterns into producing a more productive sense of order before they groove into your mind and become habitual.

We all need a sense of order to achieve. If you had a vision of being the world's greatest restaurateur, then you would need to explain what your vision looks like and find people who can help fulfil your dream. You would need chefs, waiters, food delivery etc. To achieve, you need to follow or create a system of order and communicate your vision to your team. Picking up a scrambled egg brain after it's gone south and working out how to restructure thoughts is essential when fulfilling a purpose but not impossible. Don't give up if you have struggled with Scrambled Egg Brain.

The journey of developing a healthy progressive mind needs a starting point to establish some sort of order. Learning an order of thinking is a foundation for creating, practicing, and teaching your mind to be adaptable. People with minimised thinking can also learn how to expand their thinking by managing and minimising unproductive thinking. If you find yourself being labelled with a diagnosis, take some time to explore the label before you accept it.

The Great Comparison

One of the greatest robbers of achieving a peaceful mind is thinking through the mind of comparison. Identifying what makes us feel unhappy is crucial in helping us connect the dots to achieve a more peaceful self. Have you ever noticed how much we compare as a society and on an individual level? I think it goes something like this: Have you got the latest mobile phone, television, car, house, furniture package, mortgage, best interest rates, best image, hair colour, shoes, clothes, university, social networks, titles, and so on. Oh, let's not forget branding, are you your own best brand? People aren't brands; and they have thoughts, feelings, perceptions etc. I wonder if we went a little too far on the branding bit.

Have you ever noticed yourself comparing yourself to others or something else? How about I break that down just a little? How about you take a moment to really unfold what that comparison looks like, sounds like, and feels like. Here, let me help you a little, switch off. Switch off! Switch off and learn to minimise and chill for a moment.

Take some time to think about who you are and where you are going in life. It's a lot easier to create your individual journey if you aren't comparing.

Hopefully, you've switched off a little.

What did you discover about comparison?

Why do we compare as individuals and as groups in society? What is it we are trying to gauge when we compare? Just stay with me for a moment while I offer a little descriptive insight into what comparison can sound like.

I remember many years ago comparing myself to someone who appeared to be more advanced. I remember specifically allowing myself to weigh up against the perceived success of someone else. In this process, I weighed up what I thought this person had achieved, owned etc, what I discovered was my values were not the same at all. Their accomplishments were made up of entirely different processes to mine, and their results not how I would have felt accomplished.

I remember vividly the individual who weighed on my mind until the penny dropped. That weight on my mind had a name, it was called comparison and it was starting to feel consuming. I physically shook my head and verbalised aloud, "No, I do not need to compare to myself, that person is completely different to me and I have my own path to lead." At that point I started to feel more liberated.

Suddenly the years of creative journeys, academic language, work experiences, friendships, connections, and emotions of establishment felt like they belonged to me. Suddenly my years of education were something that belonged to me, and my journey of learning was unique to me. Your thoughts and experiences are just that; they are yours to enjoy. Your years of work, thinking processes, and emotional experiences are solely yours. It doesn't matter what they look like to someone else. Your skills are yours to expand on, change, condense, elaborate on, and whatever else you chose to do with them. Quite frankly, do you need to care about someone else's achievements, especially if the person is suffering burn out, physically unwell, and lacking peace of mind? Is it worth forfeiting your peace of mind?

Comparison is potentially a positive or a negative dynamic to the soul and mind. Just take a moment to think about how unravelled you might feel when comparing. If comparison leaves you feeling like you aren't good enough, haven't achieved enough, etc then you are not alone. If comparison leaves you thinking and feeling you have accomplished something for yourself then you have a greater filtering system in what you can accomplish, and are less likely to feel consistently incomplete.

Comparison in society is a great mind divide, creating a lack of mind's peace and can become a toxic bucket of emotions. Comparison filters through our schools, our workspaces, families, social networks, hobbies, interests, etc. and can lead to a sense of dissatisfaction. Comparison can potentially gnaw at the very soul of you if you allow it to. Try a few simple techniques to help you feel calm about your accomplishments and grounded in who you are.

Write an individual list of things you have achieved and the characteristics you have developed. Hi-light your proudest moment and always remember your proudest moments are yours and don't need to be the same as anyone else's.

Understanding Satisfaction

I hope you found moments in your life very satisfying to contemplate.

I wonder if we underestimate the meaning of satisfaction. If you google the term satisfaction or look in a dictionary, you will find several meanings. Among several meanings such as contentment, happiness, joy and so on, one interpretation is fulfillment. Now, doesn't that interpretation sound awesome in itself? Isn't that worth really thinking about and how people can achieve it?

Could it be people are striving for a rewarding feeling of fulfilment? Let's face it; the world is made of many societies and utterly different from each other and with diverse needs. Many cultures, fuelled by a constant drive towards having the latest materialistic objects or position, education, money etc. have destroyed natural resources. We have cultures driven by power and greed at the risk of selling out core values. How much emphasis do we really have on being satisfied with having less? Yes, we all need a sense of purpose; however, pursuing goals needs a break too.

There isn't anything wrong with a nice or even a luxury car or a small or large house, it's the underlying drive that sometimes we may not question. What difference will not having the latest gadget, house, car, or phone have on your life? What do we really understand about satisfaction? Could it be if we don't have the latest or conform to the latest, then we have really brought into being left behind? "Yes, you're just not with it are you? Really, do you mean to tell me that if I don't loan myself up, over budget for the month to buy all the latest gadgets etc, then I'm just not with it? Are you kidding me? Seriously!" If you don't have the latest gadget or whatever it is, are you really left behind? What does that mean exactly to not have the latest or be left behind, what does that represent for you?

From the time we are young we are influenced to achieve, buy a house, car etc, but what about being influenced to develop our understanding of ourselves and others. How much of our education really goes towards developing individual personality types and how we might develop fulfilling and rewarding lives? If you are a parent with children in the education system, then you are likely to understand what I'm referring to. How much of our education system really focuses on developing character as opposed to skill? How much of our education system focusses on personality types and educational options for specific personalities? Where are our young entrepreneurs of the world, do we have enough in place for our younger generation that don't fit into Maths, Science and English? It astounds me how many young people think they need to buy a house as soon as they land out of the education system. If you're a young person consider travel, living a little, be patient as bank loans can happen at all kinds of ages and stages in life.

You may not be exactly where you want to be in life right now, but just for a moment stop and think about where you are and who you are. Seriously stop, take a break and consider speaking or thinking this very powerful phrase, "I am satisfied." I am satisfied with my cat, dog, job, career, car, house, relationship, whatever it may be just say, "I am satisfied." Perhaps you could try it, say it over and over and wait and see if a sense of peace or calm takes place. This may take a while, so be patient with yourself. If you constantly compare, you will always find yourself feeling less esteemed than you deserve. Obviously, if you are into something that is very harmful to you, then I would suggest you make plans for change immediately.

Just for a moment try and think about a time you felt satisfied, it may have been something you achieved, something you ate, something you created or something you dreamed about. Take some time to think for a moment about feelings you experienced. Was it exciting, gratifying or did you relish in the thought of contentment? Identifying what makes you feel satisfied in your life will keep the wolves of comparison in the distance.

I've created a space for you to express what that looks like or feels like for you.

The Calming Influence of Satisfaction

Hopefully you have found something beautiful, and awesome that prompts your emotions with a feeling of satisfaction. Well at least I hope you have. Now hold onto those thoughts and keep it for later. Your concept of satisfaction belongs solely to you and can be a pivotal point in anything you develop about yourself or anything you work on later in life. Let me repeat that very important point, your concept of satisfaction belongs solely to you. Take time to enjoy moments of satisfaction in life before moving on.

When you reach a place of satisfaction it's much easier to think clearer without the glasses of comparison filtering through your thoughts and emotions. Even if you are someone who has a powerful sense of satisfaction, you still need challenges in everyday life to make you feel alive. Challenges create motivation, a new sense of purpose, development of character, emotional growth, intellectual growth etc. Challenges can heighten your sense of motivation and make you feel alive. Having a sense of purpose in life always requires challenges.

Our fabulous brains are made up of all kinds of neurons and networks of cells etc. Our brain, like our muscles, still needs a regular workout. In fact, our brains need to evolve continually as our brains are made that way. Your brain needs stimulation, and frequent walks through the park of life, plenty of mental weight lifting exercises, journey through books etc. During the passage of depression, my brain felt very shut down without regular stimulation, challenge and change. I learnt to create change in as many areas of my life as possible. You may find yourself in all kinds of dynamics that you aren't able to change as you would like to. However, you can change your thought processes towards the situation. At times you may find yourself in very unrewarding and unfulfilling dynamics, however, you can create change in other areas of your life to fulfil your personal growth needs.

Learning to identify what your brain needs is important in managing depression and moving on to creating a happier you. I've never met anyone who is completely satisfied, as that would suggest an individual who has completely maxed out their ability to achieve or grow any further. I believe everything in life has room to grow, develop, mature, expand or whatever word you chose to use. I believe we are born with gifts, talents, characteristics, and life is about exploring these. Sometimes the pie in the sky is what people need to aim for to motivate change.

Take some time to think about how your mind feels when you are satisfied.

Take note of things that influence your state of satisfaction.

Is there any type of dynamic that alters your sense of satisfaction?

On numerous occasions I have observed it doesn't take long for something or someone to draw away from your sense of fulfilment. That life drawing dynamic can knock on the door with the face of competitiveness. I mention competitiveness again as it's a dynamic so many people struggle with. However, you can find great humour in aspects of competitiveness.

I'm sure you've viewed one of those Christmas movies where neighbours are competing for the most glamorised house lit up with Christmas lights. Perhaps you've watched one of those movies where neighbours compete each year to take out the street competition. Christmas decorations adorn houses and end up being the most ridiculous light display. A display complete with electric cords running all over the house and yard, leaving electricity companies hoping they don't short the street out or create a house fire. Oh gosh and let's not forget inflated Santa hanging off the roof and Rudolf tied to veranda posts desperately hoping to escape another light bulb being shoved in his mouth or worse. I'm sure you get the picture, the humorous side of two characters scheming away behind the scenes trying to outdo each other's efforts.

It can be quite unsettling listening to adults with a competitive nature. Competitiveness often rings of an individual unfulfilled with a happier self. We can sometimes be subtly caught up in someone else's life. We are suddenly consumed in what someone else has or we are consumed in the way they do things. I'm not referring to a healthy starting point where we benchmark against someone or something. I'm referring to being consumed by what others are doing. People following on social media pages and checking in on what Jo Bloggs is doing now. People are constantly checking how they think someone else's life looks so much better than theirs. Oh, go on, convince me you haven't peered over at Jo Bloggs who puts their every move and whereabouts on social media.

You know the pages I'm talking about? They read something like this. 'Oh here I am at the airport. Here I am standing next to a famous person,' and reality check is you may never cross their mind again. 'Here I am in a hotel, café, and here's a picture of my dinner plate.' Oh, and let's not forget all those precious moments lost sitting opposite someone at the dinner table in a nice restaurant because they're so busy uploading what their plate of food looks like.

Quite the overload don't you think? Why do people really feel the need to do that? What do we learn by following the success or even perceived success section of others? You might consider these questions and thoughts about people who continually live on social media, are they well-esteemed and accomplished people? Do people share to motivate and inspire change or is it the perception of success, and how they want others to perceive them? People literally pay for followers to create the appearance of being liked, popular and successful. While people are spending their time following, are they living their own lives? Are they involved in interpersonal relationships? Yes, of course I realise social media is an advertising, sharing platform etc, however, how much is too much?

Did you know that several psychology studies have questioned the nature of individuals who constantly upload selfies, yes, numerous articles have questioned these types of personalities as narcissistic? Hmmm I don't know about you but I'm not keen to follow the opinion of someone completely self-absorbed? Maybe some people are just lonely or needing constant re-assurance. Whatever the need may be, I think it states underlying feelings of not having enough or feeling enough on some level. Your self-esteem is about your thinking, your self-esteem doesn't have anything to do with anybody else. If you are thinking right now that Jo Bloggs battered your self-esteem, that's where you are wrong. Jo Bloggs may have had an influence on you by his words or behaviour, however no-one but yourself control's the way you think. Being mindful of your level of satisfaction, positions you to be grateful for who you are, what you have, your journey in life and less swayed by the opinions of others.

Having Enough

Years ago, a speaker I was listening to offered a good piece of advice, "Just take from this information what you need." Perhaps you have heard it many times? That's a good piece of advice as sometimes taking something small from what seems like a huge pile of information is all you need. Sometimes it's that one small piece of information that you can conceptualise, re-shape and make your own that makes all the difference in creating a sense of having enough.

Next time you turn on your social media pages, take note how the information can seem over whelming at times, filtering through what's relevant to you can be a quick or slow process. I don't know about you but sometimes it feels like a million magazines thrown at my head and the first, second and third page is all about consumerism and people's personal thought diaries. Scrolling through a social media page can feel like an assault on your senses.

You are not alone if you feel overloaded in information, you can feel anxious about so much information. You can feel anxious as your brain is not designed to filter a huge amount of information all at once.

In my early days of processing self-reflection, I would drive and think, ride a bike and sometimes just switch everything off. Learn to rest and imagine yourself going somewhere very peaceful. You don't need to go too far to find information on how rest is beneficial for your brain. I'll mention many times the benefits of quality sleep as not only great for our brain's down time, but the impact it has on our brains smarter decision making. Good old fashion beauty sleep also rejuvenates our bodies.

Plenty of research is available on how younger children are impacted by screen time, causing irritability and anxiety. So, there's the question, why would you not practice living with less technology? Do you really need to take your phone to the supermarket? Seriously, do you really need x amount of text messages or phone calls while you shop, sit in a café, or go for a walk? Mobile phones have become an extension of the human brain, we reach, we reach, and we reach for mobile phones instead of using our brains natural intelligence to work things out. Every time you use a calculator, google maps etc you are using less brain problem solving skills. Lack of your natural brain's stimulation will impact on your brain's health.

I remember through depression how I learnt to problem solve around lack of social connections. I lived in a small rural community and had nothing in common with local people at the time. I had to seek out people I had things in common with to learn new social skill sets. I travelled hours sometimes just to be around people I could connect with and could learn all kinds of social skills from. One of the fleeting visions of myself I hung onto at times during depression was of being a more confident person, not a reclusive person. That vision was my pie in the sky and there was the great question? How am I ever going to be a confident person from the middle of a paddock? That small vision motivated me to create a whole series of journeys to develop a more self-confident people person.

Switching off technology and asking yourself questions is good for you. Asking yourself questions can be confronting at times, but don't panic as most things in life have a solution. When your brain is overloaded, switch it off and Switch it off. What's beneficial about this process is it's free.

Mastering the Anxious Mind

I hope you feel a little more relaxed after switching off technology, noise and other distractions.

An unrested mind will turn into a flood of anxious thoughts and worry. Anxiety is a debilitating disorder for millions of people. Anxiety is a normal emotion but when not managed can have physical debilitating side effects. When you make a step forward to manage whatever you are anxious about, it decreases the level of anxiety. E.g. You might be very anxious about studying for an exam, however the moment you start to study for the exam you are managing your anxiety, therefore decreasing its impact on you.

If you're an individual who suffers anxiety, I sincerely sympathise with you. However, there is always hope in minimising anxiety and I'd encourage you to try simple things to minimise and manage it. If you need professional help, please seek help that teaches you to manage and minimise your anxious thoughts.

I suffered all kinds of anxiety in my younger years and managed both anxiety and depression without medication and professional support. It took years of managing and practicing my own thoughts to get a grip on my brain and the messages it sends to my emotions. I'm not an individual who takes medication, in fact I rarely use medication for anything. It's all about practice, practice, and practice. Some years ago, a GP offered me a script for the lowest dose of sleeping tablets as I was waking at night. What I thought I needed was a Psychologist to listen while I reflected upon anxiety and how I could quickly change it. The receptionist in the medical centre phoned back over twelve months later wondering why she had an envelope with my name on it. I laughed and told her to bin it. I'd solved the problem long ago and a few days of sleeping tablets I'd been prescribed at the time was enough to tell me that sleeping tablets weren't going to work for me.

In my perseverance to be emotionally independent, I changed my bedtime routine, minimised alcohol consumption, minimised screen time, increased intellectually engaging activities, and altered my diet. My sleep increased, my anxiety decreased and my mind calmed. As I have mentioned before, the mind is an organ that just like any part of the body it needs the right measure of self-care, regular exercise, healthy food sources and lots of happy stimulation.

I remember some years ago, thoughts of driving in a major city, being a country driver and lacking heavy traffic driving experience, left me feeling extremely overwhelmed. As I started to approach the city, the highway lanes increased in width, volume of traffic and traffic speed. As I was travelling alone and lacked another driver to change seats with or help me gain perspective on my driving abilities, I started to imagine the worst scenario of being stuck on a bridge holding up traffic. I imagined being consumed with panic not knowing where I was going, at this point my imagination discovered another gear my car didn't have. I imagined myself on the 5 pm news as the driver who had held up countless lanes of traffic. As my sweat level increased through my body and my hands felt slippery on the steering wheel, my breathing changed rapidly. At this point I knew I needed to take charge over my thoughts. I remember quickly verbalising a conversation aloud, as if someone was sitting in the seat next to me. The questions went something like this:

Question to self, "Ok so, what's the worst thing that can happen today?"

Answer aloud to self, "I don't know where I'm going."

Q. And that's terrible because?
A. "I'm worried someone will toot at me and get angry at me because I'm holding up traffic?"

Q. And will that be so bad as drivers consistently toot at people in the city?
A. "Well I guess not."

Q. And is that a reality or just your imagination?
A. "It's my imagination."

Q. And you're in the city this weekend because?
A. "I have appointments."

At this point I started to focus my thoughts on why I was in the city rather than what I was feeling. I also noticed my breathing reduce rapidness and my body shook less.

The worst fear for me was not knowing where I was going. The imaginary dialogue continued as I drove into the city.

Q. Ok, so if cars toot at me because I'm slow or I look like I don't know where I'm going or I take the wrong turn, does it really matter?
A. No it doesn't matter at all.

Q. And what will you do?
A. I'll just ignore the driver behind me. Exactly!!!

By using self-talk and practicing your imagination as if another person is present the above technique is a powerful tool. You can learn to write your own script in a dialogue that works for you.

As it turned out I was fortunate enough to have an easy flow of traffic when I arrived in the city and found my hotel without any difficulty. It took several years to minimise my nervousness when driving into the city, and it took years of practice for my nerves to subside and lots of self-talking and self-praise every time I arrived safely, and left the city safely.

You can feel anxious about many things, however, by practicing positive thought processes over time, managing and minimising anxiety is achievable.

We all need praise and positive feedback at some point in life. Self-praise is a powerful tool, however when you learn to self-praise you are not relying on others to support you emotionally or psychologically. I'm not referring to a form of vanity. I'm referring to creating conversations in your second person, for example, "Well done. You did well today to arrive at your destination without being so nervous." I have had many conversations with people who won't walk into shops or go places on their own, as anxious thoughts arise. If you have an anxiety about something, try breaking it up into small sections. Take some time to think about what makes you anxious in the situation and ask yourself questions? Is it what you think people will think of you? Is it what you fear will happen? Are you afraid of how you will feel if you don't have control of the situation? If you allow your feelings to dictate to you in these types of situations, you will limit your life experiences.

I remember vividly the day I took another step of ownership over my anxiety of city driving. I stood in a city hotel lift and was thinking about driving out of the city. I had rehearsed the conversation and spoken it many times in my mind. It went something like this:

The receptionist would ask, "How was your stay?"

I would reply, "It was great, but now I have to get myself out of the city."

That response often caused me to become very nervous, sweaty and anxious. I consciously made an effort one morning in a hotel lift as I travelled down to the reception desk, I said no, "I don't need to tell the receptionist my difficulties driving out of the city. I don't need to think about it anymore, I don't need to stand in reception sounding distressed, nervous, uncomfortable, or anything else. I don't need to check for anyone's reassurance about escaping the city traffic." I consciously chose there and then that it would all be fine. I checked out, smiled, and said, "See you next time." Although I was more than capable of driving out of the city safely by this stage, my mind had grooved a powerful thought process that told my body I would be nervous sweaty etc and something terrible would happen. From that day forward I constantly reassured myself each time I drove to the city that I would be fine.

As you practice techniques, the overthinking process eventually stops, as that's the power of your mind. Isn't this the truth about so many of our negative processes? We over think, we overplay them in our minds, we feel them in our bodies. We experience them in our minds like movies or a record that plays and over-plays, recreating a memory of negativity. A memory that eventually builds to something that feels overwhelming and sometimes just plain traumatic for us.

The good news is, we also have the capacity to reduce negative thinking processes by practicing how we perceive and how we are going to react. I do realise this all sounds quite simple, however, it's all practice and people produce results at their own pace. Do you remember something from your child- hood like being afraid of the dark, the wardrobe door open, storms, winds etc? Do you remember it fading away? People have exercised their will by using the power of their minds to manage, minimise and create more positive memories. I realise people's experiences, backgrounds, circumstances and perceptions are all very different, however a step forward can be a healthy step forward.

Another time when I shifted house into a larger town, I had a terrible panic attack while riding my bike. It was as if somewhere in the bottom of my nervous system I was desperately wanting to release negative energy and move on. I literally gasped for air as I rode my bike. I chose to keep riding and not give into the panic. Sometimes it's helpful to separate the problem from yourself. Remember, I mentioned earlier about self-talk and telling comparison to go away. Imagine reducing negative thoughts with creative descriptions.

You are an evergreen tree, dense with beautiful leaves and delicate blossoms; one of your branches starts to grow away from your trunk. It's not the change in the shape of your beautiful tree that concerns you so much; the beautiful green leaves and delicate small blossoms have turned brown. You tell that limb to shed its brown leaves and reshoot like the rest of the branches. You notice over time brown leaves starting to fall from your branch and crumple as they hit the ground below. It might take a while to shoot, but they will in due time. Eventually, your branch blossoms again with beautiful green leaves and delicate flowers. Over time you don't notice your tree shape growing with a large gap between the family of branches. You are too busy admiring the overall beauty of dense foliage and the aroma of blossoms.

Externalisation comes from the concept of Narrative Therapy (David White and Epstein). Both these men were great pioneers in the concept of teaching people to externalise a problem by naming it. The concept of naming and externalising gives less power to the problem as separate from self. E.g. "Ok panic, I don't need you now so you can go somewhere else." As I continued to ride home telling myself it would be ok and there wasn't anything to panic about, I noted my breathing changed, my body felt less sweaty and my thinking was clearer. What's important in mastering anxiety is once you start naming anxiety and telling it to go away, you need to make a choice to change a behaviour. Simple self-talk such as, "it's O.K., I'll be ok, I'm going to be ok," will become a natural part of your thinking. Practice slow deep breathing when panicked, the more you practice, the more it becomes a part of your ability to manage and minimise your perceptions in situations.

Take a Deep Breath and Chill

Whatever works for you to calm your thoughts and mind, write it down as a reminder to yourself to come back to that place when you need to.

I hope you have chilled out a little. Lets' move onto one of the most resourceful skill sets you will ever own.

SELF QUESTIONING

Take time to understand the dynamics that have an impact on your clarity of thought. Look at what you are doing, how you are doing things and who and how your influencers are having an impact on you. Self-questioning is crucial in identifying who you give access to into your thinking space and how they influence you.

A very simple list as follows may help you discover what influences your mind.

Who are your influencers?

How are they influencing you?

Do they have your interest at heart or their own?

Why did they come into your life?

What did you notice about yourself or your situation after they came into your life?

At what point did you allow them to influence you?

How do you feel when around your influencers?

Do you develop as a person or remain unfulfilled?

The Negative Mindset

It never ceases to amaze me how negative people waste mental energy. Have you ever noticed certain people automatically jump to a default position every time a situation arises? People with negative default positions are not their own best asset, let alone yours. I'm sure most people have encountered someone with a negative mindset. Often whatever you put forward or whatever the person encounters have a negative response. Let me write the script for you if you're a little unsure on this one.

"Hey Jo Bloggs, how about we do this?"

"No, we've tried that in the past and it didn't work," or, "It takes too long to achieve it," or, "No one is interested." "I like it better this way because that's the way we've always done it."

Yes, know the type? Negative people will have a whole bunch of negatives about all kinds of things and usually a whole bunch of reasons why something won't work. If you work in a group of people, it's not unusual to encounter the individual who will respond to every idea with a negative. Sadly, the negatives rule the race and perseverance doesn't get a chance to show its shiny sneakers over the finish line.

Negative people often express life through a narrow lens, limiting opportunities for personal growth and external growth. Pessimistic people find it challenging to move through challenges and changes.

Perhaps you've also noticed sometimes negative people are often physically unwell and love telling you their latest diagnosis, medications, and how they can't do something because of their illness. I wonder how much internal thought life is negative; plenty of positive people with physical challenges have achieved incredible goals in life. Perhaps you've noticed the negative personality type that always talks people down. Negative people can lack vibrancy and may minimise their activities and engagement, within communities. Yet, history is full of inspiring people who have started out with little and achieved so much in their lifetime. It's not unusual to encounter people who attempt to inhibit the progressiveness of others because of beliefs about their own lack of confidence. I could go on; however, this is about redirecting negatives into positives.

It can be very challenging to change your own behaviour, when negative influencers are constantly reminding you of how they see you. Move away from negative people until you form your positive behaviour and opinions. Let me say this very clearly about negative people, SWITCH OFF from their stuff. If you're a switched-on person or have just found a new level of being switched on or progressive or whatever word you chose to use, switch off from any negative thought processes connected to them around them or about them. Focus on your newfound progressive freedom. You may find you need to take your mind through a few processes. For example, Do I really need to care what Jo Bloggs thinks about me? Do I really need to care if Jo Bloggs doesn't think I can do this course, drive this type of car, be a better person or whatever it may be? Try developing your own thoughts. 'I'm capable,' and, 'I will,' affirmations can go a long way in building confidence in establishing your new positive thought processes and behaviours. Take your time to pinpoint negative influencers and their impact on you.

Redirecting Chaotic Thoughts

Hopefully you have chilled a little and discovered some dynamics about your influencers, whatever that looks like and sounds like to you. How about focusing on the letting go process. I'm completely aware letting go isn't as easy as it sounds, as sometimes it's a complex process. However, I hope to shed some light on some of these processes.

People talk a lot about letting things go, however, sometimes we don't think about the benefits of letting things go. Letting go doesn't necessarily mean we need to have afternoon tea with someone who has grieved us. Letting go is about managing your own peace of mind. Mind you, letting go doesn't always mean shaking hands or hugging someone who has really grieved you. It doesn't even mean a conversation with them. You can't let go of something if you are completely angry, sad, disappointed, or other emotions you may be experiencing about a situation. The process of Letting Go is to benefit you. I remember using this strategy many years ago, it was quite instrumental in pinning underlying feelings of depression. I have passed this strategy onto others who have felt very bottled up with ill emotions towards others.

I remember years ago verbalising rather loudly years of suppressed emotions out in the middle of a paddock as I rode my bike through an orchard of orange trees. I imagined verbalising my grievance to an individual and expressing all thoughts and emotions associated. It's amazing how you feel an incredible sense of release, unfortunately my release and freedom suddenly turned to emotions of shrivel as I rode my bicycle home. I realised that there was a group of workers in the orange orchids who had become privy to my conversations. Well, not to be deterred by the workers listening, I decided not to worry about being listened to, instead I decided in my imagination they all had earphones on and were very happy listening to music. I wasn't going to have my newfound emotions of release squashed. Ouch, sometimes it pays to vent when you're quite confident people aren't present.

If you've ever been to therapy, then you would know what I'm referring to is Gestalt Therapy. Gestalt therapy was developed by Fritz Perl and focussed on imagining an individual is sitting in the chair opposite you. The process is designed to address the individual in the chair and speak or act out any unresolved business you have towards that person. In my case my chair was thin air while I rode a bicycle along riverside and through orchids and wheat paddocks. My conversations would often go as follows:

"I'm really annoyed when you..." or, "Why do you always...? I feel so..."

Maybe you don't have an open wheat paddock close by or a riverside, maybe you have a room with a pillow, a pillow you can grumble, cry, or talk your feelings out to. If you have a shoulder to cry on, well that's even better. Minimising angry emotions doesn't need to be hard, it's really about conversations and the more you practice these conversations the easier it becomes. The more you verbalise or write down unresolved thoughts on paper or finding other ways to express your emotions becomes a lot easier as you practice.

If you're someone who needs something physical, then a punching bag, gym etc or thin air, the less frequent you are likely to use it as a process.

The focus of letting go of something or someone is about being free in your own heart. It's not about what someone did or didn't do to you. People move on and may not give you a thought. Now why would you give your power away right there? Let me repeat that, why would you give your power away? Why would you give your power away to someone who doesn't even care about you anymore or what they did or didn't do for you or to you? I'm not referring to legal processes here, even in legal processes, sometimes people never disclose why they did or didn't create harm. I'm sure you've read or watched murder trials in the media and still the convicted person hasn't disclosed where, how or even why they committed a crime. It's very hard to resolve in yourself if you're someone who needs details. I sympathise with you if you have been the victim of a horrific crime.

Take a moment to really think about this? Why would you allow your mind to be filled with the presence of someone or something else that has caused you harm and may not even care about you? Sometimes therapies like Gestalt are instrumental in helping people let go of unresolved ill feelings and thoughts in the journey of developing a more positive mindset.

People process letting go in many ways, take some time to think about what will work for you.

Reducing Tension and Creating Physical Calm

Unresolved feelings affect your body. I'd struggled with eating disorders for many years and major depression. I'll discuss this a little later, but what I learnt about deep breathing and being still was instrumental in resolving feelings. As I learned to breathe in very deeply while lying down, I would breathe out and feel little clicks inside my body. I would hear them; I still hear them when I need to relax. You can use this technique of breathing in and out to imagine letting go of things that clog up your emotional thought life. If you've ever been to a good massage therapist, then you know what I'm talking about when you can feel the masseur unknotting all that soft tissue. Those tiny little knots are what inhibits regular blood flow that eliminate toxins from your body. Un-knotting emotions has a very similar effect on the mind, soul and spirit of a person.

I'm sure you've encountered what people often describe as a toxic person. That's how your mind and body feel if you allow negative unresolved thoughts and emotions to clog up your person. Just like a massage that unclogs all those little tense joints in your body, so does the process of letting go of unresolved thoughts and emotions in the mind.

If you want to keep your emotions free of clutter, choose carefully who you connect with in your life. A reconnection with someone that has not developed in their own personal life, can cause you great harm or can undermine your own personal growth if you allow them to. I have had several people in my life that have created harm that I would never reconnect with, even though their own lives may have moved on, sometimes it's best to move on whatever your reasons may be.

Let me just illustrate this for a moment. Imagine you have resolved an issue about something or someone. You come across a person who knew you had a particular issue; all the individual wants to do is remind you of the issue as if it's current. Suddenly it's like feeling pushed into a corner and you are unable to move forward. The issue you have worked through is still of interest to the other person, whatever the motive may be. Learn to develop your own level of assertiveness about your own calm mind. You can develop simple responses that re-enforce your newfound freedom. For example, "Hey Jo Bloggs. Yeah that was a while ago, I've moved past that issue now." You will feel less put down by asserting your resolved grievance.

It's amazing how people you meet in life can take on your grievance, or have a desire to keep you in a state of grievance. Sometimes people don't intend to be harmful to you and sometimes people do intend harm. Don't let other people's bitterness become your problem. People thrive on other people's misfortunes, as it makes them feel better about their own misfortunes. Sometimes people clash with others because of their unresolved issues. It's important to contemplate this stage as it allows people to work out why they react the way they do.

Select your battles wisely, if the thought of fighting battles suddenly conjures a picture of people with weapons, well it's kind of like that sometimes. Words can be powerful just as much as someone's body language towards you. Some people and situations are exhausting. Learn to fight battles that you have a conviction for and that you can see a brighter future in. It takes more courage to walk away from dynamics that won't change and won't be good for you in the long run. Keeping your emotions free of clutter can help keep your physical body and self-esteem healthy longer.

Life is full of stressed out people. It's a lot easier to filter stressful situations and people's influence on you if you can ask yourself the right questions.

Why does that person have an influence on me? Do they remind me of someone? Do they remind me of a time in my life where I was struggling? Am I still unresolved about an issue?

If something doesn't sit well with you, then decide to process it and let it go.

How many times have you disliked something, or someone based on a negative experience and have allowed that experience to influence the way you perceive situations? Imagine a woman who wears her hair tied in a bun and works in a retail store. You go into the shop one day and order something you need. The retail assistant with her hair tied in a bun isn't pleasant and every time you see a woman with a bun in her hair, you automatically have a dislike for that woman. You may not even be conscious of it. Well, you're certainly not alone on this one. However, what you may be doing is eliminating the opportunity to expand your thought processes and emotions. You may have been very traumatised by something, so when your smell, sight, touch, taste, and hearing encounter a situation that remind you of the dynamics you react.

The reaction you experience hi-lights your unresolved thoughts and feelings and minimises your ability to expand in thought and emotions. So, let's just trip back to the woman with the hair bun. Somewhere in the back of your mind every woman with a hair bun is unkind, when in reality this is not true. To help resolve the situation you could say to yourself something like, "Oh well, that wasn't the best retail experience, but I won't let that affect me." Obviously if a situation has caused you great trauma, then the process may take longer.

Why do I think processing small negative experiences matter? Well your next employer, client, or someone you could have a great relationship with could have a hair bun, and subconsciously you start sending out negative vibes that could narrow your chances of something good for yourself. Somewhere in the back of your mind you've suddenly pulled forward your previous negative experience and you start to re-live it. It may not be on a conscious level but it's still affecting you.

Just a simple example, in a shop one day I spotted a woman who was very unpleasant to me when working in a previous place. My mind straight away switched to my previous unpleasant experiences the moment I spotted her. My mind slipped straight to the woman with the bun in the hair mode. Realising the salesperson now worked in the department where I wanted to buy a product from made it more unpleasant. As this salesperson pursued me, I really felt like I wanted to walk out the store. Feeling very guarded I gave the salesperson minimal information about what I needed. As the salesperson continued to demonstrate products and showed me their interest in what I needed, I slowly dropped my mental guard. I decided in the transaction that I would give the person the space to be themselves and do their sales thing. I left the store that day with two products heavily discounted and a little smarter knowing I had let a bunch of negative processes go. Perseverance paid off on this occasion, we both got what we needed. Of course, being aware some situations are more intense and require a whole of bunch of layers to unravel, my point is you can chose to make a change in your thinking. It's often small experiences of unresolved experiences that snowball.

Perseverance always produces something, if not character. Never give up as perseverance produces all kinds of results. You can change all kinds of fears in your mind, motivate yourself and learn resilience.

Whatever you do in life will require perseverance. I spent a good part of my life persevering through all kinds of struggles. I spent my first pregnancy days studying full time, working afternoon and night shifts. A long drive home from College each day and exhausted, eventually produced graduating as a nurse. My final exams were sat while breast feeding a screaming baby.

Perseverance always produces something. Battling through depression on my own was a tough set of dynamics. Living in a small rural community in the middle of the drought without talking to anyone about it was a huge risk. It was also a risk I was prepared to take to develop my own emotional independence.

I spent a lot of time in self-reflection, reading books and eventually finding things to occupy my mind. Lack of encouragement was often exhausting until I used a lot of self-talk to turn my negative thoughts into more positive thoughts. Eventually, when people came into my life that were thoughtful and kind, it had a soothing impact on me. Being watered with positive feedback about your person feels like a cactus showered with rain for the first time.

The Master in the Ear

Your influencers in life can either have a negative or positive influence on you. I'm sure many people have encountered an individual who likes to whisper sweet nothings in an individual's ears. Sometimes that's exactly what they amount to, sweet nothing. Sweet sounding words can have very little substance without actions and be very addictive to the individual who's love language is words. Sweet-sounding words can influence your thoughts and that's exactly what they are meant to do. Influential words that sound sweet can be coupled with a motive. The motive is often hard to decipher as it's so sugar coated with beautiful words. I'm not referring to the language of compliments and just being plain good old-fashioned kind. I'm referring to that strange feeling that leaves you constantly wondering what the motive is. If you're thinking right, hmmm, this woman is a bit suspicious. No, that's not what I'm referring to.

I believe some people connected to your life can leave you feeling so uneasy that it creates an emotion of anxiety, something just doesn't feel right. That feeling if you ignore it can cost you a whole bunch of stuff and loss of peace. Suddenly the decisions you make, or lack of decisions can affect your life and other's around you as your thinking filtering system has been influenced in a way that inhibits the real you. Here's a few questions people find themselves asking.

Why did I fall for that? Why didn't I see that one coming? and sometimes people don't ask at all and end up in the same or similar position. It can be very challenging at times to break cycles that are familiar to us.

Take some time to self-reflect and ask yourself some questions regarding the Master in the ear.

The Art of Empowering Self-Praise

It can take time to change self-perception, sometimes weeks, months or even years. After struggling with eating disorders in my earlier years, my self-perception felt very shattered. It took some time to work out why I had such a negative self-image. If you're struggling with a dieting or image disorder my advice is to seek professional help. Find someone who you feel very comfortable with and gently work through a healing process.

I remember working out my triggering points, I felt like I lived in an out of control chaotic habit that I desperately wanted to change. I remember mapping out what my triggers were, managing, minimising, and healing from them. One in four girls suffer from an eating disorder. It's not a pleasant journey. Just like brain self-talk, I took myself through a body love language to heal myself. I spoke lovingly to all the internal organs and muscles in my body as part of my healing process. It took some time to really appreciate my physical body. I remember praising myself each time I developed healthier habits of diet, exercise, and just general care. Some days I would wake and realise my habits had changed and eventually it wasn't something that burdened my body, spirit, and mind. You have so much power when you take ownership over what you perceive as your flaws, and I'll say that again, what you perceive as your flaws. Eating disorders are about an individual's needs. When you identify the need, you can work on how to fill the need and heal.

There is so much personal empowerment knowing that you have overcome something. It may be something very insignificant to someone else, but it may be something very significant to you that helps build your self-esteem. I would encourage you to develop a very strong and healthy sense of personal pride in overcoming something that has bothered you. Celebrate every little successful step along the way, it's your success, own it, relish in it.

Take some time to write down your thoughts that have helped you overcome something. These are your personal empowerment thoughts. These are thoughts you can draw on at other stages in your life when presented with challenges.

I spent several years after eating and image disorders, celebrating my good health. I remember thinking I'd never make it to 25 years old. Well, I'm much older now and I made it with very good health. If you have an eating disorder or body image disorder, I'd encourage you to seek support that teaches you how to manage, minimise and heal. My recovery took a long time as I chose to work through it at my own pace and not guided by professional help or social support. I spent years developing my own healthy thoughts about my body, inner thought life and how to move on with life.

In my quest for happiness, I experimented a lot with foods and my metabolism. Find foods that work with your metabolism as the right foods will help you feel good about your body. If you're wondering what, my turning point was in overcoming such serious disorders, it was often my dreams and visions connected to creativity. I started to develop a very strong inner determination to achieve my creative dreams and visions and knew I needed good health and good self-esteem.

A Ray of Sunshine

The origin of the word depression is Latin and means, "to put down." That's an interesting way of viewing things in your life that leave you feeling put down. If feelings of being put down indicate the current epidemic of depression sufferers, that sure means a lot of people feel put down. I'm unsure what percentage of people are diagnosed with depression or have experienced depression, but I imagine the numbers are still up there. I've had many conversations with people who have had depression, have depression or sadly have been affected by someone who isn't here anymore. Given the fact that sometimes people don't seek a professional diagnosis, but will seek family or work through the issue at their own pace, would add to the world statistics on depression. I can speak from experience around the feelings of being put down and how that filtered through my whole person.

I didn't seek professional help during depression, as I chose to develop assertive skills to empower physical, emotional, psychological, and spiritual independence. I remember thinking if early pioneering psychologists were able to formulate strategies and care plans, then why couldn't I? I worked out early what my triggering points were and constantly worked at managing and minimising episodes in my mind. I worked at changing my thought processes consistently. I remember reading a few good books on negative thoughts, about achieving success and decided to work on changing my thoughts. If you think I'm going to tell you I changed my mode of depression in 7 - 28 days, I didn't, it took a long time to change many negative thoughts processes and at times many small steps. As I was a nurse in my earlier career, I knew how to write a care plan, so I adapted one to suit myself. I wrote a care plan for my mind and body. I took a lot of risks for someone who lived on a rural property and didn't discuss depression with people. This was a path I chose to overcome challenges, your plan could look and sound completely different.

You can change your body's response to depression by exercising. Exercising your body regularly will make your body feel cared for and less put down by self. Learning to assert yourself socially definitely deals with feelings of being put down through ostracism, bullying and what I define as sophisticated forms of bullying. Learning to think for yourself and decision make also minimises feelings of being put down.

I remember vividly one morning waking up feeling so overly consumed with depression that I cried walking all the way to the shed to get my bike. I took off on my bike still crying. I rode until the tears stopped; I don't know why I was so distraught that morning, however, I completed my usual bike ride that day. I realised at that point that riding a bike was extremely beneficial in releasing endorphins in my brain. For almost 25 years I have ridden a bike almost daily. In the early years of overcoming my depression, I would ride different pathways to create different memories in my brain and increase my body's ability to move out of its comfort zone. I can't remember exactly how many years I suffered extreme depression, but it was many. You may have experienced people shunning you through depression and the way they reacted to you. What you will learn as your mind recovers, is that some people have little empathy and those people aren't important in your recovery.

If you're wondering why I didn't commit suicide, I'll explain it. I grew up in the religious network and being constantly told of a heaven and hell seemed terrifying. I had a belief system that if I committed suicide I would go to hell. I remember standing near the shed one morning about to go for a bike ride feeling extremely down. I had a thought if I removed a heaven and hell belief from my thinking, then how much substance as I person would I really own? That thought was one of the most insightful thought-provoking thoughts I'd ever grasped. How much substance do I really have as a human being to get myself through this? It was that morning I really started to question myself and my beliefs about my abilities. I believe as individuals we have the capacity to re-write all kinds of things in our minds and develop healthy pathways for ourselves.

The best piece of insight I can ever give you or someone you may know who struggles with depression, is Never give up hope. You never know what tomorrow looks like as any measure of positive things could happen. You can learn to move yourself through feelings of despair. Seek someone out and talk about things that concern you. Feelings of despair are different for each person.

People can choose what information they allow to filter through their mind. I won't go into the functions of the brain right now but just imagine something very simple about negative thoughts. In simple terms negative thoughts, and all kinds of thoughts, are stored in a big brown paper bag in the back of your brain. The bag is getting heavier by the moment. Without realising it the paper bag is starting to tear and the information in the bag is too heavy to carry. You know you can't carry that bag anymore without dropping all the contents. Go on, take the contents out and put them down in front of you. You can start to slowly think about those items and what you can do with them. I know this may sound very simplistic but sometimes unravelling the mound of challenges in your mind helps you gain perspective on how to move through things. Moving on is a choice and it's your choice.

I learnt to challenge my thinking from, "I'm depressed," to, "It's o.k. things will get better," and, "things will work out."

Before you accept a diagnosis of depression, allow yourself the following thoughts. Grief is often identified as depression; both have similar symptoms. Grief is a normal part of life along with sadness. It's O.K. to feel sad, flat and at times a little under the weather. What isn't healthy is an ongoing state of unhappiness, lack of direction and purpose. Allow yourself the time to explore why you feel sad or unhappy. If you have struggled with depression, you may feel grieved at times as part of your life has passed you by on certain levels. Once you identify the things you feel sad about missing out on, you can create the language to heal the voids. For example, "It's o.k. I didn't get to experience happiness like I could have, however, I look forward to happier times." Take the time to contemplate how you will make a lifestyle change to move forward. Take the time to explore a physical activity you can engage in to increase your endorphins or (happy genes).

Take the time also to explore how to express unhappy thoughts. Allow yourself some natural scenery and sunshine on your face, as nature is an amazing place to draw inspiration from.

It's amazing how alive you can feel with sun, wind, and scenery if you feel boxed in by negative thoughts. The wonderful thing about being outside exercising is it will only cost you time in your day. I cannot stress enough the importance of exercise being of great benefit to your brain's ability to reshuffle negative thoughts around, while being active or just time to think, plan etc. Sun, breeze, and scenery is beneficial for depression sufferers as it can help you feel alive again. Simply soaking up a little sun on your face increases your vitamin D, which studies have shown links to decreasing depression. Don't forget the sunscreen.

People talk about being shut down and express feelings of going into melt down. I can remember using a technique where my body felt overheated and nauseous as my mind was struggling with negative dynamics. I lay down, placed a cool face washer on my head and increased the room air flow. I imagined I had the power in my mind to move all the negative dynamics about a specific situation out of the way. Not in a harmful way, more so to gain clarity in thought.

I'll simplify this as much as possible. Imagine you have a head full of negative dynamics about people, objects, places etc. You need to go somewhere but believe the environment will be full of dynamics that are harmful for you. You really want to go to the event but feel overwhelmed. So, you imagine a draft board with all the pieces set up on it. You start to move across the board a square at a time. You start to jump pieces on the board, opposition pieces on the board are the negatives in your mind. You jump the first, then the second and so on. Eventually you get to the other side of the board. You are feeling less shut down as your mind starts to see a clearer path. Dynamics you thought were overwhelming in your mind are minimising in power. You suddenly realise you have the power to move those negative pieces out of the way. You start to feel empowered knowing you have taken charge over your body, mind, and emotions. You get up and arrive at your destination as if nothing has happened and contribute to the event and socialise as normal. You feel amazing and that's because you are.

When you walk outside you can allow your mind to take in surrounds outside yourself, allowing you to reduce negative thinking. You can develop a habit of deliberately taking in what you see outside, the trees, birds, flowers, sky, rivers, oceans, mountains etc have many moods offering tones of colour, shadows and movement throughout the seasons. Look up at the sky, take time to deliberately look up at the sky. I believe looking up at the sky gets you in the habit of looking outside of yourself and positions you to look ahead for a brighter set of circumstances.

Diet was also crucial for me in working with depression. I had watched a documentary some years earlier on studies of men in prison who were given fish regularly in their diets. While studying men in prison, researchers noticed that the aggression levels in men changed over time. Although plenty of research supports fish as brain food, I'm inclined to agree, fish improved my brain functioning, particularly moodiness.

Part of my major challenge during depression was my inability to motivate myself, focus and complete simple tasks. I learnt to recognise who, where, what and why those around me were having an impact on me. I learnt to motivate myself as I knew I wasn't going to get support from anyone around me. I spent years literally training my brain to follow a pathway and complete a task.

The process of mastering fight or flight, a theory, developed by Walter Cannon, started with what many people would consider the most tedious task. Remember I mentioned earlier about being away on holidays and deleting my email box when I returned. Deleting my emails manually hour after hour was incredibly tedious, but it helped retrain my mind. A very simple tedious task can be used as a training ground for reconditioning your mind to not flutter all over the place. It's also a very simple way of training your emotions to stabilise and not be dictated to by how you feel or don't feel when completing your goals. I'd encourage you to try something simple in retraining your mind to complete something for yourself. I've created a space for you to think about something you would like to complete.

Hopefully, you've worked on an area that needs your undivided attention. Now hold onto it as that's a reminder you can overcome something that needs a little tender loving care in retraining your thoughts into producing positive outcomes.

As I mentioned earlier, understanding your learning style is important to help you express your thoughts and emotions.

Understanding your learning style can help you identify methods and strategies to create change for yourself. It also helps you put into perspective how things look and how you can re-create things into self-empowering thoughts. Creating a description for depression can help you put into perspective how something looks in your own mind and how you can re-create it into something much more powerful for yourself. Creating a description for depression can help you recognise it when symptoms start to resurface.

I define depression as a rubber ball wound tightly with dark string. The good news is rubber bounces and with every twist of unravelling you are closer to bouncing that ball. Rubber balls bounce and human life is meant to bounce back from all kinds of circumstances. I know depression can seem to go on forever and you may think it's too overwhelming at times, but hang in there as a step forward unravelling is a step closer to bouncing that ball.

Depression always comes with a thought life of its own and it's a thought life that you can work through, and learn to minimise, and eventually master.

The following thoughts are some of the thinking patterns that need to be challenged.

What's the point?

I'll never get anywhere

I can't do it

I'm stuck

No one cares

It's too hard, I'm going to sleep

It's too hard, I don't want to be here anymore.

No one will even notice if I'm not here

My life isn't worth living.

Let me tell you right now, there is always a point to your existence. Genetically speaking, you are one in many trillions. I don't know about you but that makes me feel unique. So, if you consider your chances of being here, why wouldn't you want to find ways to make steps forward on some level? People do care, find them, don't worry about the ones that don't. Your life is worth living, you have something to offer, no matter how big or small. You will impact something good on someone else's life just by getting through. Celebrate moving out of a dark place, you deserve it. You can always achieve something if you really want to.

People generally aren't stuck; they can develop steps forward on some level in a practical sense, or even through developing positive thought processes in their mind about their situation. I'm not referring to horrific imprisonment here. History has inspiring stories of people who have suffered the most atrocious of crimes and situations and still managed to see a glimmer of hope on their darkest days and the loneliest of circumstances.

Plenty of research has been developed on depression, how to live with it and manage it. Plenty of research is also inconclusive when it comes to the effects of treatments and therapy styles. What I learnt from depression is if we only use a small percentage of our brains, then I'd develop other parts of my personality and brain functioning. I also learnt to draw on my own internal resources. Coming out of depression made re-realise how sluggish my brain and person felt. I spent time developing all kinds of skills. It would be rare for me to sleep during the day like I did in the early days, unless my body absolutely needed it or if I wanted to meditate. Sleeping during the early days of depression was a major issue for me. Sleeping for me during depression was a withdrawal, it was a withdrawal from unhappiness, boredom and lack of direction and hope. I slowly replaced my sleeping time with artistic time and socialisation. I'd reduce an hour sleep time and increase the productivity time. It took years to discover happiness, direction, and break boredom.

I worked hard in the early years of depression to engage my mind. I studied, travelled, and made new friends each time I travelled from country to city. I spent years living very isolated and travelling outside a rural region, helped build confidence and bring clarity to my person through the people I met. I was fortunate enough to encounter positive people and build good friendships because I made the effort to meet people. Being in environments with mature minded people, that weren't afraid to give positive feedback was good for my soul. Positive feedback from people helped me understand my personality type. Constructive criticism given with an appropriate tone was also beneficial and helped me look at areas I needed to improve in. I would strongly encourage you, if you have depression or episodes of depression, to be around positive people who are interested in pursuing like minded interests. As I am aware, the mental health system can have long waiting lists, seek people out through community support groups who understand and can help support you.

You can explore documentaries, books, articles etc. on cases of people who have had amazing experiences using their minds to heal their bodies, inner thought life and emotions. The results of people's own motivation for healthy mind, body, soul and spirit speaks of a better lifestyle. You may be living a better lifestyle already and fortunate enough as you have applied plenty of preventative measures including positive thinking, exercise and self-confidence. If something works for you, stick to it, and improve it.

Being prescribed sleeping tablets and taking the prescribed dose for a few days, left me feeling like the staircase in my brain wasn't attached to the top floor of my brain. Psychologist visits definitely didn't work for me. One visit with a person lacking life experience was enough to tell me I was pretty advanced in my self-analysis and the second referral, well that one as I mentioned earlier sat in an unopened envelope in reception for over twelve months. I spent time researching sleeping habits, what to change, how to change and persevered. However, we all need people at some time in our lives to help us gauge what we need and what our beliefs are in maintaining a more confident self and healthier lifestyle. Please don't misconstrue what I'm saying about professionals, medications etc, they certainly have their healing place. The purpose of this narrative is to encourage people to explore possibilities further.

The Driver of Dreams and Visions

Learn to develop imagination. Your imagination is one of your greatest natural resources. As a child I read books on inner healing and am still fascinated with people's remarkable recoveries of healing. I remember reading books on how to use imagination and creating characters that ran through my body fighting off germs and what I now know to be the power of positive thinking and healing. It's amazing how many people use their minds to self-heal from common colds, flus and recoveries from accidents, traumas etc. You can focus on the healing process itself or what life looks like for you after a recovery. Take time to explore what will work for you.

There are many therapies, techniques and possibilities out there for healing. Develop, develop and develop imagination. Imagine yourself somewhere positive that pulls your mind out of a dark space and places you on a path of pursuing something good for yourself. You may find your imagination will develop in small sections and eventually vision will become a strong part of your person.

On a visit to a city one time, a friend said, "Welcome to the Land of the Living." I often look back on that comment and think, yes,

I was not living, I was existing. You might take up the challenge to change the way you perceive yourself and the world. You might find things out about yourself and others you never knew. You might feel experiences differently and your senses might start to come to life.

When you put yourself through a whole new process, it takes you out of your comfort zone and helps shake the rigid thought processes. If there is one thing, you will be able to say to yourself, it's good to look back and know the difference between a dark space and compare it to a calm space. Another description for depression I often use is, living in a small dark room with a small window on one side and a narrow door on the opposite side. On occasions the window might open for a small time frame to allow a little ray of light in, and the door would open very quickly and close again very quickly.

Eventually I realised I had the power to create a larger door frame for myself, and could open the window for longer lengths of time to allow the sun to shine in. If you're wondering how to apply what that looks like in a practical sense, it goes something like this. Find practical things that are good for your body, find things that you are passionate about, find things that feel natural to you and you do not struggle with. Note that challenges are completely different to struggles.

Write yourself positive affirmation lists to remind yourself that there is always a ray of sunshine, eventually a little ray becomes a stronger ray of sunshine, and many rays of sunshine. What's even more extraordinary is you will see the sunshine down on you and the shadows will fade away. Catch yourself out with negative thoughts and speak to yourself, "No, I don't need to think negatively today." Feed your brain positivity, if horror movies, drama, sad or action thrillers impact on your mind, leave them alone. Find something that develops imagination and something that can give you a sense of purpose in working towards fulfilling your vision. Write lists,. create charts, try notebooks, try whatever works for you to remind yourself to use your imagination.

Understanding dreams can be part of the healing experiences. How much notice do you take of your dreams? In my experience, dreams can filter through unresolved issues and find their way from your emotions into your subconscious mind, and then into your sleep life. It's during your sleep life that your body is still and quiet. The quiet allows your subconscious mind to jump up and down saying, "Here I am, pick me, talk to me." Sometimes googling the meaning of dreams and taking a few days to think about what they represent can help you work them out. Sometimes our dreams are ridiculous and take in what our minds haven't filtered through the day.

I know my dreams became a powerful influence when I was mastering depression, as I used my dreams to explore pathways to developing healthier esteem. For example, I remember dreaming about things that hindered my personal growth, I then created pathways to achieve and reposition myself. When dreams are vivid, asking yourself conscious questions and exploring can be helpful. You can create your own mini learning lab just by exploring all kinds of dreams and what they represent to you. Now, that's a potential brain sharpener. What do you dream about? What's your daydreaming like? Here's a space for you to express your dreams.

After depression achieving can seem pretty challenging, particularly as logic and reason seem to go out the window. Its o.k. though, you can learn to lasso logic and reason back through the open window before they get too far away. Once you've lassoed these dynamics, working out dreams and visions requires a few dynamics, yep, you need resources. Resources might include people, skills, finances, opportunities, etc. We also need internal motivation, a positive outlook, perseverance, communication skills etc, we need to be able to gauge if a dream or vision is realistic? Remember that things don't always go to plan, however it's natural to feel disappointed and that's o.k. Allow yourself the time to re-think and keep moving forward. Plenty of people have started with little support in life and sometimes minimal resources. If you persevere, you may find all kinds of support on all kinds of levels.

Exchange of Language and Building Friendships

Friendships are important in life, they provide comfort, companionship, fun, sounding boards for clarity of thought, encouragement etc. A friend recently said the following: "Women greet each other with, 'You look beautiful,' and then they form friendships." That's an interesting definition of how women form friendships. Are women really that simplistic? Or is it women really desire to be told wonderful compliments about themselves to help them feel secure amongst each other?

Everywhere you go, you need to alter the exchange of language and how you deliver it to communicate what you need. For example, if you go to a bank, you speak in the language of assets, cash, borrowing, repayments etc, then hopefully you are on the same page as the bank manager and hopefully some sort of monetary exchange will take place. Anywhere you go in the world you need a currency of language, to communicate. If you travel internationally or within other cultures your language changes so you can communicate, and hopefully you are on the same page.

Now let's just slip back to that simplistic idea about women, and how they communicate, what? No wait a minute, seriously are women really that simplistic? You greet me with," "You look beautiful today, and you're my friend. Maybe that works for some individual women but what about that, "Sweet Nothing," concept I mentioned earlier? What if a group of women discover after a few short meets that the pleasant words don't quite measure up? Just for the sake of this exercise, lets' call two women Sue and Sally. Suddenly Sue and Sally don't seem to want to exchange nicer currency words anymore. Why is that? Well, women have more depth than that as suddenly Sue and Sally discover that it takes a whole lot more currency of language to form a friendship. Suddenly Sue and Sally have discovered each other's behaviour, and the currency of body language and behaviour has really kicked in and doesn't quite measure up to each other's standards or approval. Sue and Sally start knit picking at each other and oops, Sue and Sally are throwing verbal lolly bombs without the sugar coating at each other. Maybe they aren't verbalising non-sugar-coated bliss bombs at each other, maybe they just don't meet with each other anymore. Oh no, well, there goes all that nice peace and calm again on the inside. So, what if we unravelled what that distance looks and sounds like for a moment

Sound familiar? I'm sure many people have encountered friendships that just don't work. Wow! Suddenly that awesome friend who spoke beautiful admiring words that sounded so sweet and made you feel warm and fussy on the inside, isn't so awesome after all. So how do you get back to a place of peace and calm again? Well that requires a fair amount of self-reflection. Let's have a little look at that shall we? Did someone complimenting you really make you feel safe enough to form a friendship? If so, why, and how did that make you feel so secure? If your love language is words and admiring words, then your world is potentially shaped by people who offer you words of comfort, that make your soul feel warm and fuzzy.

Mind you, words can be powerful tools and very encouraging, but isn't that why so many women have been bankrupted, exploited, etc, by someone who offered warm and fuzzy words? I don't intend to sound harsh about words. What does it really say about an individual if so easily influenced by words? Let's face it, we all like pleasant words at some point, but do we need to constantly seek or rely on them?

Let's imagine for a moment, you've just gone to great lengths to put on a nice pair of heels and a great frock. You look great, you arrive at your destination and nobody says a thing. You suddenly feel your great frock style confidence drain from your body; your face suddenly starts to show more pleats than the skirt of your dress. You want to run and hide and you're wondering what's wrong with you. OOOHHH no, you forgot to build your own self-confidence, you forgot to say, "I feel good, I look great," or whatever words you chose to use. These are words you can apply not in a boastful way, but more so enjoying the effort you have made. You may need to say this to yourself numerous times before you go out on any occasion. Healthy self-esteem isn't dependent on the words of others, it comes from within. Yep, your self-esteem needs to come from knowing who you are, and looking good on the inside first.

Take some time to think about who your friends are, how you feel about them and if they impact on your self-esteem. Take some time to also think about what you bring to the friendship table.

When you recognise your mind's intelligence, you attract intelligent people and cultivate brilliant friendships.

Shifting Through the Brain Gears

Have you ever noticed the amount of jobs that ask for multi skilled people?

Imagine this for a moment, you are doing five things all at once like trying to dig a tunnel. Instead of working on one tunnel dig, you're digging five holes with a spade, hmm sounds exhausting and will probably take some time to dig a tunnel to the acquired depth, let alone five underground passages. If you focus on digging one tunnel, then you're bound to create depth, width and get somewhere a whole lot quicker.

The brain is designed to focus on one pathway at a time. When you focus on one task at a time, the brain processes things through much clearer, this is particularly helpful when re-training scrambled thoughts. Our brain functions so much easier when focused on expanding one intellectual thought process at a time and following through with methods. This process of focussing on one thing at a time helps develops depth in understanding and will help you build resilience, perseverance etc. Learn to love you brain, it's a huge part of yourself. You don't need to be overly boastful in your acknowledgement of intelligence, just a few hand rubs on your head and a little brain whispering can go a long way. Take care of your brain it really is one of your greatest asset.

The Quest of Self-Love

Yes, I know I'm sure you've heard it over and over, how to love yourself, your physical flaws, make the most of them etc. Most of the women that print those books look like a complete Glamazonian. I mentioned earlier my struggles with image disorders in my early 20's. Those years for me were horrible, I struggled terribly with self-image, body image and my inner thought life felt like a chaotic nightmare. As I started to minimise my behaviours, I started to appreciate my body, person, spirit, and intellect. It was a long journey and eventually I developed all kinds of mind tools, exercise tools and foods that worked for my metabolism. Exercising the right amount released the right number of happy genes, and an appreciation for self.

If you're someone who lacks self-appreciation and has all kinds of behaviours that aren't positive, you can learn to recognise what triggers certain behaviours by learning to start conversations with yourself. Therapy will only do so much for you. It's up to you to accept or change how you perceive you. I'll talk more on this another time, in short, I learned to identify my triggers, change my perceptions, and filter that through my physical body self-care.

It's important to like how we look physically of course, in my quest for self-love, the purpose of physical features like hands, face, feet, are important for movement and expression. You can develop a respectful care for your internal organs, muscles etc by what you eat, drink and how you exercise. Society has placed so much emphasis on not just the physical appearance of people, but also how people should be perceived. It can be disheartening listening to someone run off a list of what they don't like about themselves, both physically and on a personal development level. You can work on this area of yourself. People can be great self-haters and sadly resent others who have what they think they don't have.

If you're wondering right now if the question, "Does my butt look big in this?" was on my list, not all, many well-known individuals made their claim to fame on rounded behinds. I'll leave that question for those individuals past and present. The reason I mention physical appearance is because people gain a first impression of you by your grooming but most importantly the expression on your face, especially a smile. What's relaxed is a smile, I understand sometimes it's hard to smile, depending on circumstances. However, a smile is an expression people will always remember about you. Smiling also relaxes your face and is linked to research around endorphins being released when we smile.

Prior to my journey of self-appreciation, my internal thought life was filled with terrible self-doubt. To help you appreciate yourself and understand yourself more, you can try questions like the following:

Why do you doubt yourself?

What could make a difference for you to have more confidence in yourself?

Does it really matter what others think of you?

Does it matter if the opinions of others aren't what you expect?

Do you believe you can acknowledge you on a greater level?

Most importantly in self-questioning, do you like who you are? There is nothing more fulfilling than waking everyday knowing you are someone. The core of self-acceptance has nothing to do with a title, material possessions, popularity, how smart you think you are or aren't, purpose, achievements, etc. These things are results of your journey. The core of self-acceptance is knowing you are someone and the rest you can pursue. If you are gifted with compassion, empathy, listening ability, kindness, encouragement etc. develop the gifts that make you feel alive and connected to people, and of course animals.

As I grew older my negative thought life and behaviours around physical image changed. My internal thought life expanded into a deep appreciation of self.

If you're wondering right now if I'm one of those people that has little sticky notes all over my house, to reinforce positive self-concepts, the answer is no. I believe the more you tell yourself something positive, the more natural it becomes as part of your belief system. If you chose to believe you're the most beautiful, intelligent, or kindest person on the face of the Earth, you do that, you go for it. Who is anybody else to tell you otherwise? Self-confidence is a highly regarded and great asset for anyone.

Overcoming disorders, graduating from nursing with a newborn, while working afternoon and night shifts and long drives home is enough to tell me about the power of the mind. Years later, running a household, a cattle business, studying a degree and various other creative projects is also enough to tell me I am experienced and skilled at organising chaotic thoughts and overcoming many challenges.

What you overcome in your lifetime to achieve something is one of your greatest resources. You can use your accomplishment and all it took to get you there as a pivotal point for years to come. Imagine you've lost your direction and don't know if you can do something. You have lots of self-doubts and suddenly find yourself coming up with an amazing amount of excuses why you complete something, or it just won't work. Often the first thing people can do is verbalise an extensive list of negatives out of their system. E.g. I don't feel like I can ..., I'm frightened, what if it doesn't work? What's the point? etc. All these negatives are good to verbalise so you can gain perspective by self-listening or by someone else listening.

Take some time to think about a time you accomplished something, or experienced something that you never thought you would get through. Yes, it was a challenge wasn't it? You probably cried, laughed, got angry, frustrated but you arrived in the end, didn't you? Now that's your pivotal inner strength, you learnt resilience in that experience that you probably didn't know you had. You learnt perseverance, you learnt how to manage life as it was thrown at you, like someone standing in a restaurant kitchen throwing dinner plates at you as they came out of the washer, expecting you to catch them quickly. Just like a pile of plates you managed though, you did it, you got to the end of it didn't you? You're stronger than what you think, more organised than what you think, you might not have had a cheering squad telling you how great you were and what you could do, however looking back did you really need it?

It's a lot easier to achieve when you resolve accumulated negative thoughts before starting something new. However, sometimes things pop up as we progress through life. Resolving is different for everyone, conversations could sound as follows:

"Ok, so that's what Jo Bloggs did to me that really upset me, I can't change it. However, I can choose to move on from it and I can work at being my own best person."

"Ok, not everyone will like you, however if you like yourself you might find you will naturally draw people to you. You might discover you will naturally gravitate towards people you like that reflect something of yourself. You might even want to hang out with people who are the opposite of you as self-appreciation goes a long way in accepting others."

People always talk about finding their path, direction, purpose etc. You are already born with attributes and characteristics. Develop those attributes and characteristics in places that challenge them. If you don't know what they are or have lost them through years of depression, anxiety etc. Just think about pivotal points in your life where you spent time on things and what you were doing? Did you use your hands making things? Did you interact with animals, read books, play sport etc. Often these activities give indicators as to what comes natural for you. If you've never engaged in activities, then I encourage you to explore, take some small steps and try some new things to develop the new you.

That's not to say your life won't be void of challenges, however, managing your thought processes will make your journey more satisfying, knowing you have overcome or reached another milestone in your journey. Celebrating your accomplishments, however big or small, in whatever shape or from reinforces your perseverance. Own your accomplishments, celebrate them as they belong to you. Most importantly, celebrate you as I mentioned earlier, you are one in so many trillions.

Simple Re-affirming Thoughts

As I mentioned earlier, your brain develops what many professionals refer to as fight or flight. Over time your brain develops reactions to all kinds of scenarios that remind you of previous experiences. Take some time to really think about this. Just for a moment think about the last time you felt anxious. Have you tried creating a conversation around this or writing it down? You may find a deep breath just to help you relax right now might help you clear your thoughts.

I've had many conversations with self that have sounded as follows:

"I'm really worried about ..."

"I think that this or that might happen ..."

"I feel like ..."

"What if ..."

Have you tried to pinpoint each thought and feeling and had a conversation around it? I realise not everyone will self-conversation and that's O.K, as sometimes another soul to listen can be very beneficial in helping you gain perspective.

Remember earlier the conversations I mentioned about driving to a city? Working on conversations that can help you rationalise and head towards positive thoughts, can help filter through feelings of nervousness, fear, inadequacy etc.

It's quite common for destructive behaviours to follow thoughts of anxiety. Try and work on breaking cycles in small steps. For example, you might feel anxious about meeting new people and burst into tears, or not go out as you fear people's reactions. Try very small steps that build your confidence and separate yourself from the anxiety. I can remember in my early 20's being so shy I would burst into tears. I boldly practiced reading in class and volunteered for radio programs. Why I'll never know, as radio can be very challenging as you need to imagine your audience is present and listening. Also, in my earlier days of being terribly shy I practiced talking to cashiers in supermarkets, a simple "Hi, how are you," always opened the way for simple conversations.

On the odd occasion, I'd encounter a person who really wanted to talk to me, it terrified me as I didn't feel I had much dialogue to offer. Eventually talking to strangers became natural. My earlier thought processes went something like the following:

Learn to imagine yourself in positive situations, doing positive things.

Practice re-affirming positive thoughts

It's o.k. I can do this

It's ok that people might stare at me

It's ok that people might laugh at me if I make a mistake

It's ok that I try when many people don't

It's ok because I am achieving my personal goals in doing this.

After repeating these types of conversations, eventually my brain recognised that I could change. You can try similar dialogues or write your own. You can speak all kinds of positive things to yourself, your body and mind. The brain has incredible power to change the way you perceive yourself.

Make yourself simple re-affirming phrases. For example.

I can

I am

I will

'I can,' re-affirms your ability. 'I am' re-affirms your positive self-perception, 'I will,' re-enforces your action.

Music Fulfills and Motivates the Soul

Music has much to offer your soul. Our souls need stroking with affection as much as our mind needs care. Have you noticed how certain types of music can influence your mood or change the atmosphere? Music is a powerful tool for heightening, energising and calming emotions. Minor notes have the capacity to sadden the emotions. If you are inclined to depression, or bouts of sadness, play music that lifts your mood. Listening to sad music while depressed or sad only feeds the sadness. If you love listening to lyrics in songs, find lyrics that are interesting, happy thought provoking or fun. Some religious organisations play music with minor notes to change the atmosphere, often before communion or the traditional alter call. Religious cults are notorious for this, the change of atmosphere takes a person into a saddened or serious moment. Saddened moments leave people most vulnerable, particularly when it comes to decision making.

When you walk into clothing stores, especially clothing for the younger generation, the music is often upbeat, louder than usual and adds to the funky shopping experience. Supermarkets in previous times played elevator music, you know the type of music that leaves you feeling like you have all day to just gently wander the isles slowly stacking your grocery cart without a care in the world. If you feel anxious, listening to music that calms your mind and relaxes you is beneficial. If you explore the internet you will find mediation music coupled with beautiful images of nature and void of lyrics. The images are designed to take your mind away to beautiful landscapes of oceans, forests, mountains etc, and switch off from the stresses of the world. Mediation music can bring to the surface unresolved emotions as it stills your mind, and allows your emotions to speak to you. Our spirit absorbs music and sometimes not even on a conscious level. Listening to music, that resonates with you can be inspiring and change the way you feel and perceive things.

Music has been used in therapies, is a global language and is a powerful industry that changes lives. Music can remind you of specific times in your life and how it influences your state of happiness. You can explore your thoughts connected to music by asking yourself what you were doing, where and who you were with, to understand how to create happier moments for yourself.

Whenever I hear certain songs playing it reminds me of singing lessons I took some years ago. The lessons and singing experience were valuable, the songs remind me of all kinds of feelings and thought processes. I also noticed my memory had increased some years later, as singing is connected to releasing stress and improving brain health. Music provides release for all kinds of emotions and is fulfilling to the soul. Take time to understand music that motivates you and has an influence on your emotions and how it influences your thought processes.

Increase Your Imagination

Using your imagination is an exciting concept; without imagination you would find it extremely challenging to achieve. Without it, it's challenging to motivate yourself as you need to be able to visualise yourself accomplishing your goals. The internet, books, journals etc. offer all kinds of research on imagination, how it works and which part of the brain it originates from.

Some experts talk about neurons as networkers in the brain, and research can identify those light bulb moments. You know those moments when someone is talking about something that happened and suddenly you can visualise what they are saying? You do the, 'Aaah, yeah!' response. That's your visualisation kicking in because you have memories stored in all kinds of compartments. Your imagination is when someone says can you imagine ..., and your mind suddenly starts creating all kinds of concepts. Does everyone have imagination? Apparently not, as some people are known to have Aphantasia, a condition where a person lacks the ability to visualise in their mind. Don't rush there yet if you can't visualise or imagine yourself doing something, all kinds of things influence our creative ability to visualise. You can think of imagination as your problem-solving solution and fun creative zone.

Sometimes we just need to clear out all those energy blocks to let our imagination run free, oh and I'm not referring to imagining the worst for yourself in any given situation.

When was the last time your imagination had a run through the park of life, created something awesome or produced something amazing as a result? What did that look like?

You can do things to increase imagination, such as less television at night, reading and working with mediums that stimulate your senses. The right side of the brain thrives on imagination and opens the way for innovative ideas. Why wouldn't you want to expand your thinking? Seriously, does the thought of the same routine day in, day out for the rest of your life really excite you? Can you imagine at the end of your life telling your loved ones you did the same thing day in, day out, year in year out? Imagine the possibilities of what you can achieve in life, where you can go, travel to or how you can expand your social connections? Your social connections can stimulate your imagination, sensory experiences, add laughter and most of all provide good company.

Imagination feeds your soul, spirit, and body. Imagination prompts us to physically get up, explore our options and start a new day. Where do you imagine yourself today, tomorrow or maybe a week from now?

A lot of society, and I'm generalising here, know that we are made up of body mind and spirit. We live in an age where we have strong spiritual cultures and thousands of religions. I've read many books over the years on spirituality. I grew up in a religious network and I've got to say, organised religion just isn't my thing. However, I believe it can be beneficial to have beliefs outside of yourself, as having faith and thinking outside of yourself helps externalise and connect with greater power, therefore minimising the focus on our own problems. If you aren't focused on yourself all the time, you are potentially more inclined to contribute to others around you. Mind you that doesn't mean you need to be a martyr and give your skills and experience away for free. That wouldn't be in your best interest for others or yourself, eventually you could burn out and that's not good for anyone.

You may believe in a Higher Power or tap into groups of people with lots of energy. Whatever you chose to believe in, your spirit needs food just like your body and your mind. I'm a firm believer that when it comes to group involvement, that it needs to work both ways. You need to gain something of benefit from a group culture, as well as contributing to the culture of the group.

I believe in the creator of the heavens and the Earth. I don't think we are the only life force in existence that's for sure. I also believe some people are good for our spirits. People with healthy spirits are pro-active, non-judgemental, positive, energetic, and calm under pressure. People with healthy spirits have a life force that radiates positivity and leaves you feeling very energised. Spiritual people mediate, they look for quiet spaces to download their source of higher power, whatever that looks and sounds like is an individual journey. Learn to appreciate you and what you have on a personal level. You can make all kinds of changes to make a more confident you. Life can be very short as time gets away on us, and it's important to make life an enjoyable journey as much as possible. Consider this, genetically speaking, there is only one you and you are unique for many reasons. Take the time to explore your uniqueness.

If you have struggled with racing thoughts, egg brain, anxiety or lived in a dark place, you are most definitely not alone. Never give up hope, dark thoughts can change as you have the power to change them. Don't take note of the negative influencers who condemn your behaviours or the way you think. Find people in life to help support making a better you. Most importantly, learn to switch off, self-reflect and switch it all on again with positive thoughts.

Life's challenges can seem overwhelming at times. However, life is also full of happy moments that you can learn to create and enjoy. Learning to develop a more peaceful mind, happier thoughts and smarter you are possible.

The brain is one of the most dynamic organs and influences parts of your personality. Learn to love it, switch it off for it's down time and switch it on again with clearer thinking. Learn to identify unproductive internal thought life and activate your spirit into a strong determined spirit that overcomes personal challenges.

I learnt to switch my brain on after years of depression, anxieties and eating disorders without professional support, medications, and minimal social support. Within a five year period, my left-brain functioning productivity increased, resulting in five years of academic study, the management of a live stock business and two community roles. My right brain functioning increased with production of over 300 fabric designs, ability to produce paintings quickly and various additional creative projects. A peaceful mind enables you to function under elevated levels of stress and take steps in the best direction for yourself. It's all about managing, minimising then creating a more positive you. A step in a direction is more hopeful than no step at all.

www.youre-smart.com

www.ingramcontent.com/pod-product-compliance
Lightning Source LLC
Chambersburg PA
CBHW071530080526
44588CB00011B/1620